NIGHT

NIGHTTIME

marina hope wilson

Cooper
Dillon

Nighttime

Cooper Dillon Books
San Diego, California
CooperDillon.com

Cover Photo by Noah Wilson
Cover & Interior Design by Adam Deutsch

Image on pages 22-23 come from onlinestarmap.com
ISBN: 978-1-943899-19-7

For my father.

Table of Contents

Nighttime: the time between evening and morning; the time of darkness.

Enjoy Your Worries

Tomorrow begins
the chemical spill we'll make
do with and call survival.

On the phone, I want to say something light.
You should see the blossoms
on Charles Street. They glow in
late afternoon, but you've always been
more root than crabapple bloom.

Spring can be so brash, so boastful.
But come and sit in the sun
with me anyway.

Walking past a mirrored building,
I think of you. The world
without you in it. I wouldn't
recognize my own face.

Interim

In summer, we head to the mouth of the river
so my father can test his new wetsuit and fins before
swimming across Tomales Bay. We go inland of the seals,
and as he trudges through the shallows

and goes deeper, two seals swim near him,
eyes peeking above the surface. Later
we walk to the jetty, watch people as they
admire the waves crashing, again and again.

My father, under his breath, says,
*Look at that dumb hippy scrambling around
on the rocks.* And I have to laugh
at the truth of it, water rushing

over the man's naked ankles
to his knees. Only a fool would dare
get so close and for what—
It's only the edge

of everything, and we've been here
a long time—letting the dark
water pummel us, salt spray and
wind telling us who's boss.

It's not news.

Language of Dominion

Perhaps those maps are beautiful, too.
Vibrant cities growing inside you.

What do we dare call
progress? This advancement.

My brother drew boats and planes and
faces with deep set eyes on the old blueprints.

Foundations, property lines, numbers
landing under his sketches,

in the language of dominion.
The only imperative is to build.

Push and work and repeat.
Eat when you're hungry.

And drink. Just don't shrink.
There's no time to be still.

Expand into what little space you have.

Industry

Some parts burn

    bright.

Brain, heart, bladder
    humming.

Not red, but white light.
Hot spots so alive,

such machines
for making,

you can't see
    anything

    else.

Survival

Everyone says
you're a fighter. I imagine
they don't know what
else to say.

Isn't everyone
a fighter? Wasn't it you
who taught me that?

Road Trip

In the desert, barbed
by palms, we talk about the lifespan
of trees, puncturing the sky
with their sharp blades.

What is erasable here?
Anything can disappear. Be
disappeared.

This confetti, this light.

Shelter

The birds have flown away.
The sky tips with the weight
of their wings turning all at once.

My father's bones are the beams of a house—
Once someone said you could live there,
turn the lights down, light a fire.

Transit

In the blue city,
the stars don't affix
to any one body,

but shoot up
the spine, expanding
infinitely.

I have always thought
about the color blue
more than is advisable.

That crippling vastness—
the ocean, the sky, a
version of forever.

Remember—I'll meet you there
anytime. It doesn't have
to be lonely.

Time

Naturally, we think about stars—
echoes of old stories,
maps of places we won't go.

Upon Learning the News of My Father's Quite Certain Disappearance from Earth

At least you live nearby.
At least the hills are still green.
At least it's beautiful there.
At least you can run through the woods.
At least it burns only at the edges.
At least you have brothers and sisters.
At least you don't have kids to tend to.
At least you have a cat.
At least you have a bit of time.
At least you have someone to hold you.
At least you have a body.
At least you have some youth left.
At least you're built of blood.
At least you're from the sea.
At least you can dance.
At least it doesn't hurt yet.
At least you're tough.
At least you've traveled.
At least you wear a mirror in your heart.
At least you have skies to look at.
At least you're part star.
At least you can see them most nights.
At least that's the future-past
or the past-future or
some idea of forever or
now to hold onto.

We Have the Same Heart

Knobby knees, muscled calves,
large forehead, brown eyes
with only a hint of eyebrow.

Same flare of anger,
only mine is mostly quiet
and turns in like a splinter.

I never learned how to stomp
and throw my arms in the air.
I don't know how to be so big,

demand all the attention in a room,
be the gravitational pull. The terrifying
force of my will at the center

of everything.

Holbox Island

Anything can happen again
or never again. It's a trick of living.

Making various imaginary teas from
ocean water, we've nearly mastered
the art of doing nothing but moving
our bodies through time and space.

Her shoulders bounce along on a small pink bicycle.
We try not to measure our minutes, but mostly fail.
Look how low the pelican flies toward the surface
of the sea. Miracle dinosaur.

I'd know the sound of those sandaled feet anywhere.
And ask to hear them approaching always.

Cinematic Refrain

There is, of course, the theme of death,
clouds floating in a blue sky,
the body and what it holds
and survives
and what it cannot.

This inescapable body.
This transitory body.

A bird, a nest, an egg.

Perspective

I didn't have the heart to tell you
I didn't recognize you walking
along the side of the road.

I stopped a hundred feet later
and turned around to see you there
before reversing the car.

Who is that man,
plotting property lines
on a Sunday morning?

Once, you were a tree.
Now, we are both so small
in this valley surrounded by green—

vanishing.

Goat Rock

Heading to the coast, you're
miserable. The tight, winding
roads, flanked by redwoods, soften
into curves, now hills, cows grazing.

I watch your face shift,
eyes scan the landscape.
Open. On the verge of pleasure.

Hand to Your Mouth to Stop the Rain

He wasn't afraid of being misquoted
but, instead, of having his words

lined up like fine crystal. He thought
they would steal his soul by

listening, capturing him completely.
The quality of silence choreographed by

absence. What they call a heavy silence.
Not everyone can tell a good story.

Describe the naked men walking
along the river's edge. The heat

of the stones under their feet—

Painbirds

More and more the body becomes
a container.

Let's swim in fantasy blue.
Feel light.

The sound of your voice, even
from far away, sounds

exactly as it should. I want to ask
just what are we made of anyway,

but am afraid.

Late Summer

The scent of burning wood
is controlled, they say.
Nothing to be alarmed about.

A chainsaw buzzes in the distance.
Wind shifts through the limbs
of trees. You can hear it now—

Everything breathes.
The birds have stopped singing.

Any place can be lonesome—
even this house, full of

everything you built.

Driving Lessons

Grief is an invisible skin. You
wear someone's life in your own.
Even the way I parallel park is him.
For a mediocre driver, I'm pretty good.

Crank the wheel one way,
then the other at the midpoint.
You have to go all in or know
when you've botched the geometry.

Commit or start over.
No, that's not right either.
Grief is closer and further
away. Always both.

The Dark

He spells my name with an *e* instead of an *i*,
asks if 12 p.m. means day or night.

Everyday knowledge slides away.
He's leaving before he leaves.

Lights out at six, lights out all the time.
So what if the world ends, so what

if the cities drown. Put your coat on
in any weather. Your preoccupations

become you. Eat the same breakfast
each day. The buttered toast is sour,

but nothing tastes the way it did.

Thanksgiving

The moon is nearly full, and rainwater
falls in heavy droplets from the redwoods, madrone.
Each sound shimmers in darkness.
It has stopped raining for a few minutes.
It's perfectly nighttime here.
My father is breathing. This most salient fact.
Right now. He is upstairs, breathing.
In the world he built, this house on a hill in the forest.
This place. Our breathing together in it.

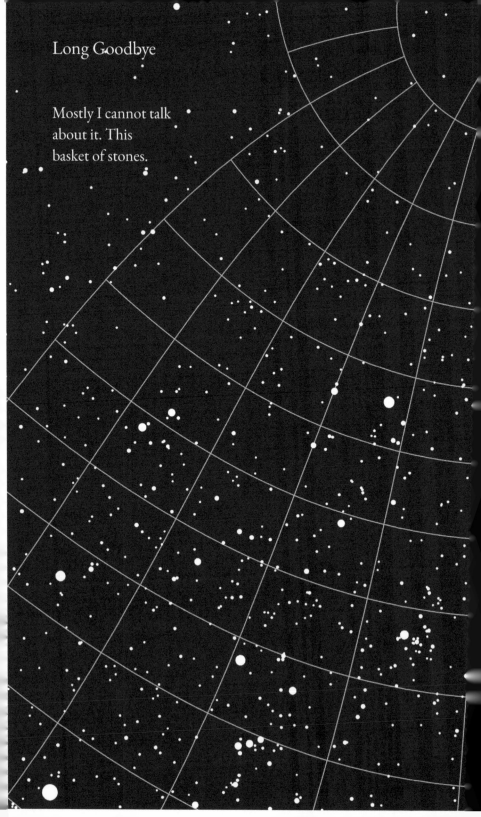

Long Goodbye

Mostly I cannot talk
about it. This
basket of stones.

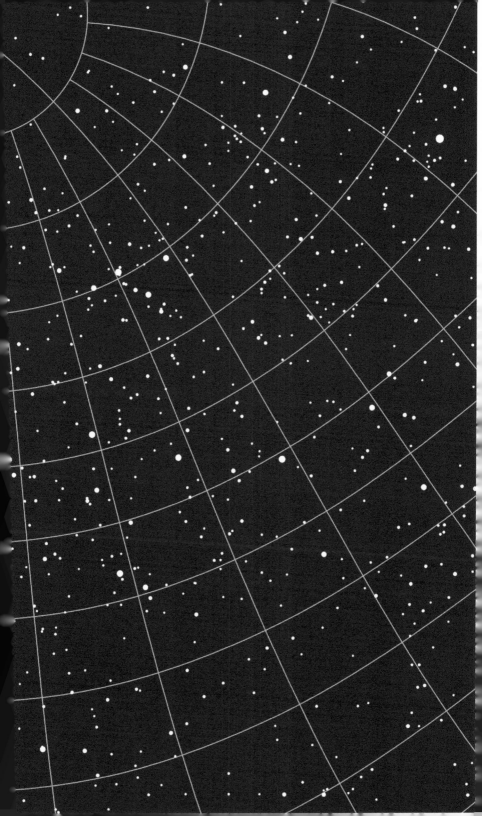

A Response

From the recliner, you look at me and say,
What are you writing? I lie.
Doing some research. I'm not writing.
The truth is I'm shopping for a purse and
embarrassed to admit it. It's so frivolous.

What can I say to you?
Once all dirt and work. Now bones and belly.
That I'm a body full of pain. That I'm not strong
enough to face the minutes between us.
That I hardly write these days.

That I'll remember that exact, beautiful question
for as long as my mind has questions.
What a cruel curve, this sickness that ribbons
your brain. Yet I'm here as you turn
to me to ask.

I'm writing you into and out of this world.
I'm writing this net to carry you.
I'm writing a tree spreading under and over
the earth. I'm writing water to fill
the empty spaces. I'm writing
the words we won't say.

Inheritance

Always bring a pocket knife,
cash, a carpenter's pencil.

Pack the points of a compass
in your head. Carry matches,

learn to swim. Not only
for survival, but to live.

Portal

Wedding muslin, a fishing hat, a guitar.
Handpicked flowers, redwood fronds.
The ornery ginger cat only you could
love keeps distance now. The dogs too.
A kind of softness in the air. A quiet.
Sometimes John Prine. Sometimes
chatter, then quiet again. Also
sunlight. A rocking chair. A tune
your son strums. The green
crocheted blanket with flowers.
Your favorite color. A photo
of your child self, and later,
with your brother at a party.
Children come in and out.
Yours, theirs.

The Drive

When I was young,
the hills were green like this

and you were strong and
unyielding as the hills—

green and full of
stories. Wet and fresh

as anyone equipped to live
in a car or under the sky.

You fought a man
much bigger than you

because he had drowned a kitten
in the river, and you said

anyone who would do that
had to be weak.

You, pure sinew, all
impulse and overflowing

with rain and green, like that.
Yes, like those hills just there.

I can see them now.

Tying

I feel an outline of myself
most of the time. A ghost.

A shadow. A kind of
echo. Or witness.

In the garden, working twine
around the branches of the

leaning rosebush, my finger
slips on a sharp reminder.

Blood rises in the delicate way
it sometimes does. Almost beautiful.

Pain can also be this way.
Feel the cool marine layer

mixed with sunlight, the birds
chirp and flit into late afternoon.

One odd side effect of grief:
I no longer feel alone. Not ever.

Earthlings (Trouville-sur-Mer)

Everyone wears nautical stripes
like a national uniform. Forty children
charge the sea, splashing and screaming
with abundance. They fizz in the water.
I'm sitting on the sand with
the seagulls who called out all
night through the open window.
Today is overcast. My eyes skip across
the water and catch the neon sails,
and beyond, gray industry. What
a wonder to be any place. To walk
on sand. Even the one limping gull
makes its way. The last time we
went to the ocean, you stayed
in the car. I rolled down the windows,
and you looked out. For a long time
like that—at the birds, the sea.

Landscape on the Train

A large white bird rests, nestled
in a tree. The fields unfold greenly—
streams and sunflowers and cows grazing.
A small golden fox crosses a yellow
stretch of land, its tail hanging
behind it. Then I see.
I am your eyes now.
You gave them to me.

Dream

He walks down the middle of Lakeview Avenue.
Nothing to see here. Just a regular living man.
Jeans and tee shirt, a flannel button down, like always.
Not dying. Not sick. Not howling. Not out of his mind.
Walking down an ordinary street, which happens to be
my street. My ordinary father, in the ordinary light.

Acknowledgments

I'm grateful to Cooper Dillon Press, and to Adam Deutsch for giving these poems a life in the world.

I'd like to thank the editors of the following publications in which these poems first appeared:

Mulberry Literary, "The Drive"
$, "Holbox Island"

Thank you to Online Star Map for allowing reproduction of the map on pages 22-23, which represents the stars at 38.467156° N 122.951052° W on March 15, 2019, the date of my father's death.

Special thanks to Noah Wilson for agreeing to a night trip to the forest we grew up in to take pictures for the cover.

These poems grew from my love for my father and the love of the land and its creatures he instilled in me and in my siblings. The area in West Sonoma County, where so much of my own and my father's story have transpired, was once inhabited by the Southern Pomo, Coast Miwok, and Wappo Peoples, and was stolen by European colonizers. It is my wish that these poems honor the land, animals, and Original Peoples of this place; past, present, and future.

I am forever grateful to the poets who closely read these poems and helped them become: Jenna Cardinale, Michael McNally-Costello & Aracelis Girmay. Endless thanks to the ecosystem that holds me together. Your conversations and your questions. Your pushing me forward insistently: Lisa Ascalon, Hillary Casper, Joyce Domanico-Huh, Lynn Edisen, David Flores, Ellen Hagan, Jessica Heidt, Zoe

Kalionzes, Michele Kotler, Marissa Kunz, Danielle Levin, Colin MacNaughton, Peter Mann, Megan McDiarmid, Carrie Paff, Jane Rinard, Jeremy Sabol, Angela Sebastiani, Bhavna Shamasunder, Sally Shannon & Tim Wright. My Celestials: Helen Elizabeth Ruth, Gabrielle Ramona Cran & Little Man Wilson.

I'm thankful to my siblings: Morgan, Steve, Shawn, Noah & Josie, all of whom shared the wild experience of growing up with my father. I'm thankful to my mother, Cecile Lusby, and my stepmother, Sara Wilson, who've always encouraged my writing.

To Mark & Priya: Thank you for being my everyday. Thank you for carrying me through so much.

Thank you to my father, Dennis Wilson. The world without you in it. Is less so. I will forever remember you standing on the deck of the house you built, overlooking the redwoods. I am not me without you. I will never be me without you.

Marina Hope Wilson's poems have appeared in journals such as *The Massachusetts Review, Mulberry Literary, Kissing Dynamite, Jet Fuel Review, $, The Racket,* and *Bodega.* She won the 2023 Rash Award in Poetry for her poem, "Origin." Her poem, "Dilemma," was nominated for the 2023 *Best of the Net Anthology.* Marina lives in San Francisco with her husband, stepdaughter, and three cats, and makes her living as a speech-language therapist.

Milton Keynes UK
Ingram Content Group UK Ltd.
UKHW041856090224
437493UK00004B/207